Amazon Rally

Eduardo Amos and Elisabeth Prescher

Level 1

Series Editors: Andy Hopkins and Jocelyn Potter

1.1 What's the book about?

1   Look at the picture on the front of this book. Which country is this story about? How do you know?

Italy	Japan	Mexico	England	Brazil	Russia

2   What do you know about the Amazon? Which of these words are going to be in this book? Write ✓ or ✗.

- ✓ tree
- ◯ village
- ◯ rain
- ◯ Indian
- ◯ jungle
- ◯ hot and wet
- ◯ shop
- ◯ dark
- ◯ cold
- ◯ taxi
- ◯ green
- ◯ train

1.2 What happens first?

Look at the pictures on pages 1 and 2, and the words in *italics*. What do you think? Which is the right word?

1   The two young men are *friends / brothers*.
2   They are *English / American*.
3   They race *motorcycles / cars*.
4   They are going to race across a *river / jungle*.

'Look, Brian! Those are our **motorcycle**s!' David says. David and Brian are at Heathrow Airport in London. They are motorcycle **race**rs from Enfield, a small town in England.

They usually race in England, and in European countries, but this time they are going to Brazil. Racers from many countries are going there, too. They are all going to race across the Amazon **jungle**. Brian is reading a newspaper.

motorcycle /ˈməʊtəˌsaɪkəl/ (n) I am going to go to France on the back of my friend's *motorcycle*.
race /reɪs/ (v/n) Twenty people *raced* down the street and I arrived first.
jungle /ˈdʒʌŋɡəl/ (n) It rains every day in the *jungle*.

1

'Listen to this, David!' he says. 'There's a problem in the Amazon. The Indians are very angry because **miner**s are going into the jungle. The miners are taking their homes.'

But David isn't listening to Brian. 'The race is going to be good,' he says.

'Yes ... and difficult, David.'

Two days later, the racers are in Brasilia. Brian and David are there, too. A lot of people come and watch. It is a beautiful, sunny morning.

There is a lot of noise. People are talking to the racers. Photographers are taking pictures.

miner /ˈmaɪnə/ (n) Her brothers are *miners* and they never see the sun.

2

'The race is going to start,' a young man says. 'Listen.'

'Good morning!' a man says. 'This is the start of the Amazon **Rally**. Forty-two people are going to race from here to Manaus.'

'Are you OK, Brian?' David asks.

'No,' Brian answers. 'I've got a problem. Look! **Oil** is **leak**ing from the **engine** of my motorcycle.'

'Where's that **glue** for oil leaks?' Brian asks.

rally /'ræli/ (n) People in the *rally* drive across the Sahara for days.
oil /ɔɪl/ (n) Can you put some *oil* in the car, please?
leak /liːk/ (v/n) Why is there water on the floor? What is *leaking*?
engine /'endʒɪn/ (n) There is a problem with the *engine* in my car.
glue /gluː/ (n) The children are making hats from newspaper. Have you got any *glue*?

The racers are putting on their **helmet**s.

'Here, try this,' David says. He gives Brian some glue. Brian puts some glue on his engine, but it comes out very slowly.

'Quickly, Brian! The race is going to start,' David says.

But oil is leaking from Brian's engine.

'Quickly!' David says again.

The oil stops. Brian puts on his helmet and gets on his motorcycle.

helmet /ˈhelmɪt/ (n) We are going into town on our bicycles. Where are the *helmets*?

4

The engines of the motorcycles make a lot of noise.

'The race is starting,' David says.

'Let's go!' Brian says.

The Amazon Rally starts!

The first day is OK. The roads are good. The racers see many small towns and **village**s. People stand near the road and watch them.

village /ˈvɪlɪdʒ/ (n) We live in a small *village* near a big town.

On the **second** day, the roads are not very good. Two Italians, Luigi and Enrico, are in first and second place.

On the **third** day, the racers are in the jungle. The roads are very bad. The Brazilians are in first and second place now. Then come Luigi and Enrico. David and Brian are behind the two Italians.

The race always stops late in the afternoon.

'Those Brazilians are very good, and they know the road,' Brian says that evening.

'The Brazilians aren't a problem. The rain is our big problem. Look!' David answers.

second /'sekənd/ The first film was good, but I didn't like the *second* film.
third /θɜːd/ The *third* bedroom on this floor is very small.

Day 4

This is our second day in the jungle. A difficult day! The rain never stops and the road is very bad. There are trees across the roads. Sometimes we can't stay on our motorcycles.

I am first in the race now, and David is second. The two Italians are behind us. We are happy about that.

It is seven o'clock now and it is very dark. The days are very hot in the jungle, but the nights are beautiful.

David is in bed. I am going to bed, too.

2.1 Were you right?

Look again at Activity 1.2 on page ii. Are your answers right? Then put these words in the sentences.

Brian and ¹ .....David..... are from England. They are in ² ....
for a motorcycle ³ .... Before the race, Brian has a
⁴ .... from his engine. David gives him some ⁵ ....

The race goes from Brasilia to ⁶ .... and takes them
across the ⁷ .... It is very ⁸ .... there in the evening
and the days are very ⁹ ....

2.2 What more did you learn?

Finish the sentences with words on the right.

1

1	Forty-two people	A	many small towns and villages.
2	The racers see	B	make a lot of noise.
3	On the second day	C	two Italians are in front of the Englishmen.
4	The roads	D	are going to race.
5	The engines of the motorcycles	E	are not very good.

2

1	The Brazilians	A	the days are very hot.
2	Rain	B	know the road.
3	Luigi and Enrico	C	is a big problem.
4	In the jungle	D	at seven o'clock.
5	It is very dark	E	are Italians.

2.3 Language in use

Look at the sentence on the right. Then put the right word in the sentences.

> 'Forty-two people are going to race **from** here **to** Manaus.'

| in | on | from | near | across | to |

1 David and Brian are ......from...... Enfield.

2 They usually race .... England.

3 They are going to race .... the jungle.

4 In Brasilia, people talk .... the racers.

5 Oil is leaking .... Brian's engine.

6 Brian puts some glue .... the leak.

7 People stand .... the road and watch the racers.

8 The roads are bad. There are trees .... the roads.

9 It is their second day .... the jungle.

10 Brian writes about his day. Then he goes .... bed.

2.4 What's next?

What problems are Brian and David going to have in the race? What do you think? Talk to your friends and write answers here.

....

....

....

....

....

....

....

....

....

The race starts very early on the third day in the jungle.

In the afternoon Brian and David stop. The jungle is very beautiful, but they aren't looking at it. They are looking for the town of Una-Una.

'Where are we now?' Brian asks.

'I don't know.'

'Is this the road to Una-Una?'

'I don't know,' David says again.

'Where are the racers?' Brian asks. 'Can you hear them?'

They stop their engines and listen.

The jungle is quiet. Then they hear a noise.

'Listen, David!' Brian says.

'What is it?' David asks.

'It isn't a motorcycle,' Brian answers.

Suddenly they see some men. They are walking to Brian and David.

'Look at those men, David!' Brian says.

'Who are they?' David asks.

'They aren't racers, David. They're ... Indians!'

The Indians come and talk to Brian and David. But the two young men can't understand them.

'These Indians are very angry, Brian. But why?'

'I don't know. I can't understand them.'

'We've got a problem, Brian,' David says.

The Indians take the two young men to an Indian village. A woman with blue eyes comes and talks to Brian and David.

Her name's Astrid and she's German. She lives in the jungle because she's working there with the Indians.

'Who are you?' the woman asks.

'I'm Brian, and this is my friend David.'

'Why are the Indians angry?' David asks.

'Are you miners? The miners want this place. Sometimes they come here and they **kill** the Indians,' Astrid says.

'We aren't miners. We're motorcycle racers,' David says. 'We want to go to Una-Una.'

Astrid talks to Maoni, the Indian **chief**. Maoni listens and talks to his men. They aren't angry now.

'The miners are coming to the village,' Astrid says. 'Chief Maoni knows that. They're going to kill his men.'

'Let's get the police, Astrid,' Brian says.

'How? There's no time.'

'I can go to Una-Una. There's a police station there,' Brian says.

'But you don't know the road to Una-Una,' David says.

Astrid and Chief Maoni talk again.

'Caruak is going to go to Una-Una with you tomorrow. He's Chief Maoni's son, and he knows the road,' Astrid says.

kill /kɪl/ (v) The animals *killed* two people because they had no food.
chief /tʃiːf/ (n) We talked to the *chief* about his people's problems.

12

At seven o'clock in the morning, Brian and Caruak get on Brian's motorcycle. Caruak isn't very happy. He doesn't know about motorcycles.

The Indians watch them. Brian starts the engine, and Caruak gets off the motorcycle quickly. The Indians run to the trees.

Astrid talks to Caruak. Then he gets on the motorcycle again. The Indians watch from the trees.

Brian starts the engine again.

'Go!' David says.

Brian and Caruak take the road to Una-Una.

It is difficult in the jungle. But Brian is a good racer and Caruak knows the road. He knows every river and tree in the jungle.

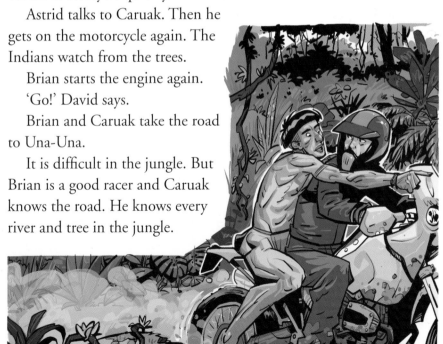

3.1 **Were you right?**

Look again at your answers to Activity 2.4. Then finish these sentences.

1 Brian and David look for the road to Una-Una, but they

....

2 Some Indians talk to them, but Brian and David

....

3 Brian and David aren't miners, but the Indians

....

4 The miners are coming to the village and they

....

5 Brian and David want to get the police, but they

....

3.2 **What more did you learn?**

What comes first? Write the numbers, 1–5.

(1) **A** Brian and David stop in the jungle.

( ) **B** They hear about the Indians' problems.

( ) **C** They meet a German woman.

( ) **D** Some Indians take Brian and David to their village.

( ) **E** Brian and Caruak go to Una-Una.

3.3 Language in use

Look at the sentence on the right. Then write sentences about the pictures.

> They **are looking** for the town of Una-Una.

Astrid .....is talking.... (talk) to Brian and David.

Chief Maoni .... (smile) at Astrid.

Brian .... (start) his motorcycle.

Caruak .... (watch) Brian.

An Indian .... (run) to the trees.

Caruak .... (sit) on the motorcycle.

3.4 What's next?

What do you think? Circle the right answer.

1 Brian is going to have a problem with ... .
   a his helmet   **b** his engine   **c** the police

2 Caruak is going to stop the oil leak with ... .
   a a fruit   **b** glue   **c** water

3 The police are going to go to ... .
   a Manaus   **b** Brasilia   **c** the Indian village

4 The Indian chief is going to give ... to Brian and David.
   a knives   **b** Indian names   **c** hats

5 Brian and David are going to arrive in Manaus ... Enrico and Luigi.
   a before   **b** after   **c** with

Early in the afternoon, they come to a big river. Brian looks in his road book. They are near Una-Una now.

Then Brian looks at the engine.

'Oh, no! Oil is leaking from the engine again!' he thinks. He stops the motorcycle.

'I haven't got any glue? Where's David's glue?' he thinks. 'This time I've got a big problem!'

Caruak looks at the oil. Then he

walks to a tree and takes a green fruit. He puts the fruit on the hot engine. The leak stops.

'That's very good,' Brian says. 'Thank you, Caruak. Let's go.'

They start to drive again. The oil often leaks from the engine, but Caruak stops it with the green fruit every time. They arrive in Una-Una in the evening.

They meet **Captain** Silva at the police station, and Brian talks to him.

captain /'kæptən/ (n) I can see ten footballers, but where is the *captain*?

'The miners are coming, Captain. They're going to kill the Indians,' Brian says.

'You're right, young man. We don't have much time!' Captain Silva talks to a policeman. 'Let's go to the Indian village. I want twenty men. Quickly!'

They get to the Indian village late in the afternoon.

'Let's wait for the miners,' Captain Silva says. 'Go behind the trees.'

It's night again. They are all waiting for the miners.

'Look!' Captain Silva says. 'They're coming.'

The miners are coming from the jungle. They're moving very quietly. There are a lot of miners in the village now. They are looking for the Indians.

The village is quiet.

Then Captain Silva says, 'This is Captain Silva. Don't move!'

The miners run, and the Indians run, too. They make a lot of noise.

Two miners find David and catch him.

'They're going to kill me,' David thinks.

But then two policemen run to him. 'Stop!' they say. 'We're policemen.'

In the morning, Chief Maoni and his people are very happy. A lot of Indians are dancing.

Chief Maoni has two beautiful **necklace**s in his hands. He smiles and gives a red necklace to David.

'*Jaguari*,' he says.

'He's giving you an Indian name,' Astrid says. '*Jaguari* is a small **jaguar**.'

Then Chief Maoni gives a black necklace to Brian.

'*Manauê*,' he says.

'Quick runner,' Astrid says.

Brian gives his helmet to Caruak.

'**Champion**,' he says.

They all smile.

necklace /'nekləs/ (n) That is a beautiful *necklace*! Was it expensive?
jaguar /'dʒægjuə/ (n) *Jaguars* live near the river, but we never see them.
champion /'tʃæmpiən/ (n) He always arrives first. He is the *champion*!

Captain Silva takes Brian and David to Manaus. The racers are there.

There are photographers, too. They are taking pictures of the champions - Luigi and Enrico, the two Italians.

'Brian? David? Hello!' Enrico says.

'Look. We're the champions,' Luigi says.

'**Congratulations**!' Brian and David say.

'Are you OK?' Enrico asks.

'Now we are,' Brian says.

Brian and David talk to Enrico and Luigi about the Indians and the miners.

'You're champions, too,' Luigi says.

'Yes, they're champions of a very important race,' Captain Silva says.

Brian and David look at their Indian necklaces.

'Congratulations, Manauê!' David says to his friend.

'Congratulations, Jaguari!' Brian says.

congratulations /kənˌɡrætʃʊˈleɪʃənz/ You are eighty years old today? *Congratulations*!

Talk about it

1 **Work with a friend.**

| Student A: | You are Brian. You are at the police station with Caruak. Talk to Captain Silva about the problem at the village. |
| Student B: | You are Captain Silva. Listen to Brian. Ask questions. What are you going to do? |

2 **Work with three friends.**

| Students A and B: | You are Enrico and Luigi. Talk to Brian and David. Ask them about the race and their problems. |
| Students C and D: | You are Brian and David. Give Enrico and Luigi your congratulations. Answer their questions. |

Write about it

You are Brian. Write about Day 5 of the race. Put these words in the sentences.

| interesting | hot | champions | miners | happy |
| necklaces | Manaus | beautiful | too | |

Day 5

We are in ¹ .... now. It is a

² .... town on the river, but it is

very ³ ....

Enrico and Luigi are the ⁴ .... of the

Amazon Rally. I am very ⁵ .... for

them. But David and I are happy for Chief Maoni

and his people ⁶ .... The

⁷ .... didn't kill them. And now we

can go back to England with our

⁸ .... and our new Indian names. We

had a very ⁹ .... time in Brazil.

20

What do you know about the Amazon? Work with two or three students and find the answers to these questions. Look at books or the Internet.

a How long is the Amazon River?

....

b Which countries does the Amazon River run across?

....

c Name three important towns on the Amazon River.

....

d Which of these animals live in or near the Amazon?

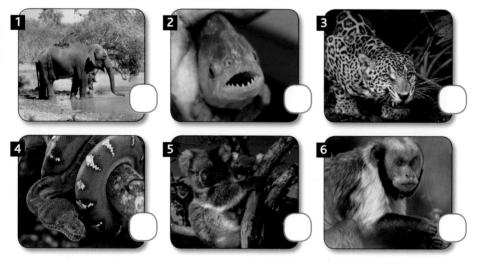

e How many Indians live in the Amazon jungle?

....

f What problems are there for the people and animals in the jungle?

....

....

....

....

....

21

2 Talk to your friends about their answers. What can they teach you about the Amazon? Write here.

Notes

3 Now write about the Amazon River and the Amazon jungle.